THE VERBALLY ABUSIVE RELATIONSHIP

Breaking Free, and Discovering a Sense of Who You Truly Are

EMILY WALKER

INTRODUCTION

The signs of verbal abuse are numerous and can be difficult to detect, especially if you are on the receiving end. But first, let's establish the context. Verbal abuse is difficult to define because it can range from 'harsh and insulting language used to upset the person being spoken to' to 'language and behavior designed to erode the listener's self-concept and bring them under the speaker's influence and control.'

The first definition is quite broad and covers a wide range of situations, including one-time incidents in which someone shouts insults at another in the street for throwing litter on the ground. In fact, by this definition, anyone can engage in verbally abusive behavior if they are under stress or in physical pain.

The second definition is somewhat more precise, implying that there are repeated occurrences over time of a wide range of language patterns and actions that profoundly affect the listener and change them on a deep level so that they become submissive to the speaker. It also implies a desire to dominate others on the part of the speaker. This book will examine the latter setup.

Signs of verbal abuse in a marriage

The following is a list of signs of verbal abuse in a marriage, but it can also be applied to any relationship in a social setting, at work, or at school.

- Do you get called derogatory names?

- Does your partner curse at you?

- Do they frequently say things that make you feel bad?

- Do you hear the same insults over and over, even if the idea is the same but the words are different?

- Does your partner frequently yell and shout?

- Do they have a bad temper?

- Do they 'lose it' over seemingly insignificant or unreasonable things?

- Do they make disparaging remarks about your job, hobbies, or achievements?

- Do they criticize your friends and family to the point where you start spending less time with them?

- Do you have repeated arguments about the same issues?

- Do they seem not to understand your viewpoint?

- Do you ever get confused in conversations with them and end up agreeing with them or giving in to whatever they want?

- Do they criticize your body, hair, or appearance?

- Do they make you feel as if the relationship would be much better if you could change or be different in some way?

- Do they make you feel inferior by mocking or shaming you in private or in public?

- Do they portray themselves as superior, smarter, or more deserving than you or anyone else?

- Do they dismiss your ideas or beliefs?

- Do they criticize you but you're not allowed to criticize them?

- Is there one set of rules for them and another set for you? Is your partner setting all of the rules?

- Does your partner 'forget' things they've done but remember everything you've said and done?

- If you are offended by their remarks, do they retaliate by accusing you of being too serious, too sensitive, or unable to take a joke?

- Whenever they see you happy do they say stuff to take the wind out of your sails?

- Do they know exactly how to set you off? And they can do it so coldly and cruelly?

- Can they ever make you feel truly happy? Have you noticed that the good times are becoming increasingly scarce?

- Even when they're criticizing something you did or said, do you feel as if they are actually attacking you, who you are?

- Does your partner provoke you and then blame you for your reaction?

- Does he or she say horrible things and then claim that you misinterpreted them?

- Can your partner twist and distort any complaint you may have in order to portray themselves as the victim?

- Do you get told what to do and what you want instead of being asked?

- Is your partner telling you that they know (better than you!) what you're thinking and feeling?

- Are you subjected to the cold treatment as punishment, even though you are not allowed to do that?

- Is it really that bad when they give you the cold shoulder, as if they aren't even thinking of you?

- Does your partner appear to take pleasure in seeing you suffer?

- Are you often reminded of "bad" things you did, but your partner decides what "bad" is?

- Do you rarely get credit for anything?

- Have you noticed that you are frequently put in situations where you are damned if you do and damned if you don't?

- Does it appear that your partner enjoys arguing?

- Does your partner say they do things "for your own good"?

- Is your partner secretive about stuff, but you have to reveal everything, where you were, who you met, what you did, what your thoughts and feelings are, and so on?

- Are you held responsible for everything that goes wrong, even if you believe it is not your fault or is beyond your control?

- Are you rarely, if ever, asked how you're doing?

- Does your partner appear to disregard or dismiss your feelings?

- Does your partner deceive you? A lot?

- Do they try to persuade you that things happened when you know they did not? Or persuade you that something did not happen when you know it did?

- Do you sometimes or frequently doubt yourself?

- Are you threatened with punishment if you don't do what they want?

- Do they threaten to end the relationship?

- Do they threaten to leave and take your children with them?

- Are you told that their bad behavior is simply a reaction to what you did?

- Do they minimize their bad behavior or even claim it was nothing?

- Do they make decisions without consulting you, but you need their approval to make any?

- Are you punished for breaking the rules even if you weren't aware of them?

- Does your partner become envious and/or throw tantrums when you spend time with, or even talk to, others when you think there is no need for it?

- Do you have to account for your spending?

- Do your children go through the same things you do? Or are they ignored?

- Do you see your husband be this marvelous, wonderful person in public, commending others and making them feel good (about him!) but then turn into an abusive tyrant behind closed doors?

- Is the majority of child rearing left to you?

- Does your partner constantly ask for small favors, keeping you very busy?

- Do they have a tone of voice or a 'look' that tells you you're in trouble and you should just do what they want?

- Do they tell you that you are a failure?

- If you become angry, does your partner become ten times as angry, implying that it is better for you to simply stop and give in?

- Does your partner sometimes not even have to tell you what they want because you 'just know'?

If you identify with many of these signs of verbal abuse in your relationship, chances are you are also suffering from the effects of this abuse. As strange as it may appear, one of the consequences of this type of abuse is that the victim often fails to recognize the abuse. One reason for this is that the abuser often redefines what a behavior means. For example, when an abuser comes to pick up his girl after a night out with the girls, she might not realize that he is exercising extreme control over her because the abuser has convinced her that he loves her and is concerned about her safety. In her mind, his collecting her is simply a way of caring for her, and there is no harm in that. She may initially be unable to recognize it as a controlling, abusive act on his part.

If you are unsure about the above list, go over it with a trusted friend (not the person you suspect of being an abuser!) because it is often easier for people outside the relationship to see the toxic nature of what is going on than it is for the victim to recognize the indicators of verbal abuse. This is not a criticism of the victim; it is simply a result of the cognitive distortion that occurs in anyone who is subjected to psychological abuse.

So let's take a closer look at the effects of verbal abuse.

The Effects of Verbal Abuse

To begin with, an environment with numerous signs of verbal abuse is a high-stress environment. Even when the abuser is not present, the victim is constantly under stress. The victim is constantly on the lookout to ensure that they do not do or say anything that will upset the abuser. This hypervigilance indicates that the victim is constantly on edge, 'walking on eggshells,' with every moment organized around the abuser and ensuring his or her comfort.

The victim of all of this verbal abuse is usually experiencing a roller-coaster of emotions. The victim may be elated, in love, thrilled, or even euphoric in the early stages of the relationship. But when the bad behavior kicks in, there are also terrible lows. As the relationship progresses, the roller coaster's highs become less frequent and less 'high,' while the lows become more frequent and even deeper. When a victim is down, they usually wish and hope for more good times to come. Because the victim is frequently led to believe that the lows are the victim's fault, the victim often strives to please the abuser in order to get them in a good mood so that things can be great between them again. And yet no matter how hard the victim tries, it never appears to be enough to satisfy the abuser, because they always find something to complain about.

The abuser purposefully causes these emotional ups and downs. As a result, the victim is thrown off balance and unable to think clearly. When emotions are high, it is difficult to think logically and rationally. That is why abusers make people feel good at the beginning of a relationship (as well as to hide their true nature, of course). When a person is in love, they have no sense of problems or difficulties and will even disregard warnings from family and friends about the new partner.

As humans, we tend to gravitate toward pleasure and away from pain. I am aware that there are exceptions, that some people enjoy pain. However, there is often a code for the submissive person to use in such situations to let the dominant person know that they've had enough, and use of the code brings things to a halt. There are no such safety measures or ways for the victim to stop the torrent of abuse in situations where there are numerous signs of verbal abuse, as we are discussing here.

In these situations, the victim often uses emotional reasoning to make decisions. This means they make decisions and make judgments based on how they feel. If it feels bad, they do not do it; if it feels good, or has the potential to feel good, they are motivated to do it. In this way, the abuser employs a reward and punishment system to exert control over their victim's actions. What happens is as follows: the victim thinks about doing a specific thing. However, they are reminded of the last four or five times they did it because the abuser went insane and it was extremely unpleasant. To avoid upsetting the abuser, the victim decides not to do it. Instead, the victim chooses to do something neutral or pleasing to the abuser in the hope that life will become more pleasant.

There are some important facets to this setup. The abuser may never say, "Don't do this behavior," but the victim realizes that doing so brings the abuser's wrath down on them, so they avoid it. These unspoken rules, or implicit rules, can be very powerful and manipulative as the abuser can always say, "I never told you not to do that," which is true. They never said those exact words. Their actions, on the other hand, send a much more powerful and long-lasting message.

The second aspect of this system is that the victim feels that they're making their own decisions. The victim believes that it is his or her choice whether or not to do the particular thing. When you look at the big picture, it's clear that the abuser has a big influence on the decision. In other words, the abuser is teaching the victim how to make decisions and how to behave in relation to them.

The abuser not only manipulates the victim's emotions, but they also have a direct impact on their thinking and beliefs. All of that mocking of ideas, scoffing at the victim's opinions, arguments about the same things over and over, criticism when the victim expresses a desire or want, not enabling the victim to criticize, all of this is designed to change and distort the victim's thinking. The abuser may also redefine words or forbid the victim from using certain words. These tactics also limit the victim's thinking.

On top of that, the manipulator frequently exerts control over the victim's behavior. The abuser usually puts pressure on the victim to act in certain ways. They could be influencing the victim's clothing, hairstyle, diet, how they use their money, how they spend their free time (if they have any!) and even how much sleep they are allowed. This last point is crucial. When a person is tired, it is nearly impossible to resist mentally, making the victim far more susceptible to being controlled and manipulated. It's actually quite common for abusers to limit victims' sleep time, and they have a variety of reasons for doing so.

So we can see that the abuser has control over the victim's emotions, thinking, decision making, and behavior. This adds up to a lot of changes, and the abuser is effectively changing the victim's personality. Family and friends of the victim frequently comment that they no longer recognize the victim, that they have changed significantly. Many books on verbal abuse discuss the victim losing themselves in the relationship, no longer recognizing themselves, or experiencing identity issues.

This is what they're talking about. The victim has basically had a false personality imposed on them. The abuser has installed this pseudopersonality in the victim so that the victim is the type of person the abuser wants to be around. The pseudopersonality has been programmed to believe what the abuser says, to prioritize the abuser's needs and desires, and even to ignore its own wants and needs. The pseudopersonality has been programmed to be very dependent on the abuser, needing permission, checking everything with the abuser, and in many cases, the personality is so blended with the abuser's personality that the victim needs the abuser to know who they are.

All of these things are symptoms of verbal abuse, or what the victim feels while in an abusive environment. However, if you are on the outside looking in, such as if you have a family member or friend who you suspect is in an abusive relationship, these may be the only signs of verbal abuse that you can see because you are not privy to what is going on behind closed doors. My point is that if you notice any of these signs of verbal abuse, do not ignore them! It is a mistake to believe that your friend or family member will leave when they are ready. The victim is not able to make the decision to leave. They would have done it a long time ago if they could. Nobody wants to be mistreated. Victims have a great deal of difficulty leaving an abusive situation, and they frequently require assistance, so speak up... to the victim, not the abuser.

Signs of verbal abuse - the pseudopersonality

It is not normal for someone's personality to change in a relationship, especially if it occurs without their knowledge or consent. Of course, in a normal, healthy relationship, a person may alter some of their behaviors or come to believe some of the same things as their companion, but this is done voluntarily, either to compromise or because it benefits both parties. This is not the same as a situation involving verbal abuse.

The concept of the pseudopersonality is extremely useful in explaining and comprehending what happens to the victim. The abuser basically unfreezes the victim's personality, changes it, and then freezes it in place as the pseudopersonality. This false personality suppresses and dominates the true personality, resulting in the person having two competing personalities. This is not the same as having multiple personality disorder.

These two personalities clarify the inner conflicts that victims frequently describe in verbal abuse situations. One part of them wants one thing, and the other part is unable to do it they are unable to resolve the conflict. For example, the person may want to leave the relationship because they are unhappy (the true personality), but the thought of leaving fills them with dread and anxiety (the pseudopersonality). The fear and anxiety they feel at the prospect of being separated from the abuser can be so strong that they end up staying in the relationship for years.

Or something alerts the person to the fact that there is something seriously wrong with their partner (true personality) and that things are not right, but the victim is not able to recognize the inconsistencies between what the partner says and what they do (pseudopersonality). The pseudopersonality is so programmed to believe that the partner loves and cares for them that they are unable to recognize abusive behavior from the partner. This may seem unbelievable to those who have never experienced verbal abuse or mind control, but it happens. It's also what happens to individuals in cults. Their thinking has become so twisted and distorted that the world in which they live has very little to do with reality and everything to do with the world created for them by the leader. The cult leader and the verbal abuser both use mind control techniques to dominate and control those around them.

The pseudopersonality is also programmed to blame itself for everything that goes wrong. Being told a thousand times that something is true will have that effect! The victim is also not allowed to take credit for anything that goes well. This is extremely damaging to the victim, and the combination destroys a person's self-esteem. In normal situations, we congratulate ourselves on our accomplishments and blame our failures on external factors. This enables us to feel good about ourselves even after failing at something and trying again later. This protective mechanism is not allowed in a verbally abusive situation, and the victim is blamed for everything bad, including the abuser's faults and difficulties, resulting in low self-esteem.

The pseudopersonality is programmed to defend the abuser to outsiders too.

The abusers

Many abusers suffer from a personality disorder, such as antisocial or narcissistic personality disorder. This implies that they could be psychopaths, sociopaths, or narcissists. It can be shocking if you didn't already know this!

It's worthwhile to learn more about this because it's crucial. The key point here is that these individuals have no conscience and a massive ego. They are not always serial killers. They either don't have emotions or have very shallow emotions. There's no guilt, shame, embarrassment, remorse, fear, love, or regard for others. They don't feel remorse for anything they do. That means they can do whatever they want and not be upset about it. They lie, cheat, abuse, hurt, and destroy other people's lives with no regard for the consequences. Their motivation is to control and dominate others.

If you are in a relationship with a psychopath or a narcissist, there are some things you should keep in mind.

It can be difficult to recognize that your partner is a narcissist or a psychopath for the same reasons that verbal abuse is hidden from the victim. Add to that the fact that most people are unaware that there are people who have no emotions, plus it may appear to you that your partner does have emotions, and you have a situation that will take some time to come to terms with.

Psychopaths do not change. The only change you'll notice is an improvement in their ability to manipulate you.

They are skilled liars. You can't believe anything they say.

A person who is involved with a psychopath loses. Even if you believe there is a benefit, it does not outweigh the harm they are doing to you.

You are better off out of the relationship, but leaving is difficult due to the dependency they instill in you. (You're NOT codependent!)

Leaving isn't enough. You must also undo the pseudopersonality, because as long as you have it, you are an easy target for the next psychopath you encounter. A manipulator can immediately identify the pseudopersonality's behavioral patterns. In fact, you might as well have it tattooed on your forehead that you were once in a traumatic situation.

The signs of verbal abuse - some myths

In articles and books about the signs of verbal abuse there are various myths or errors in thinking that I would love to mention.

The first is that individuals who value and honor themselves would not tolerate abuse. Remember how the manipulator disguises themselves at the start of a relationship in order to trick the victim into getting involved? This means that anyone can be caught by a psychopath or a narcissist. It has nothing to do with whether or not you respect yourself. I do not believe anyone allows another to abuse them. When the abuse begins as described above, there is no stopping it, no matter how much self-respect you have.

The same can be said for the notion that only those who are gullible or have low self-esteem are caught. This is nonsense, and it just blames the victim. Again, anyone is vulnerable, and the onus is on the abuser, the person who's actually hiding and deceiving the victim, not the victim, who has no idea what is going on.

'The individual is making their own decisions, and they'll leave the abusive situation when they are ready, or they must enjoy it if they stay.' This notion demonstrates a total lack of understanding of mind control and psychopathy. Anyone who believes this doesn't understand the amount of control the manipulator has or the strength of dependency the abuser has created in the victim.

'In order to recover, you must be willing to change and forgive both yourself and the abuser.' The issue in verbal abuse situations is that the abuser profoundly changes the victim. Thinking that the victim must adapt to these circumstances is counterproductive. The trick, as we've seen, is for the victim to stop changing in response to the abuser's desires and actually undo the changes so that they are able revert to having their own personality dominant. In terms of forgiveness, why should the victim forgive themselves when they have done nothing wrong? And forgiving the abuser is not a requirement for recovery. Some things are unforgivable, and the harm psychopaths and narcissists cause to their victims may be one of them.

It is commonly stated that abusers have difficulty expressing their emotions or that their emotions manifest only as anger; for example, if they are nervous, they become angry; if they are afraid, they become angry. Or that the bullying or abusive behavior masks a deep sense of inferiority, shame, or another issue. While this may be true in some cases, it is most likely a very small percentage of cases. These explanations are common among verbal abuse victims in order to explain and comprehend what is happening to them. (As humans, we like to have justifications and reasons for why things happen.) When victims come up with these ideas to describe their situation, they are not considering psychopathy or personality disorders because they are unaware of them.

It appears that those who write these things are not considering psychopathy either. According to studies, a high percentage of abusers have personality disorders. These people are defined as having a "lack of concern for others' feelings, needs, or suffering; lack of remorse after mistreating or hurting another" or "inability for mutually intimate relationships, as exploitation is the primary means of relating to others, including by coercion and deceit; use of intimidation or dominance to control others," among other issues! Needless to say, this drastically alters the situation. Dealing with a psychopath differs from dealing with someone who has difficulty expressing their emotions. When you see signs of verbal abuse, failing to consider this possibility is asking for trouble.

It is also a myth that people who have been abused in the past seek out another abuser. This is yet another method of blaming the victim. Nobody seeks out an abusive relationship, especially if they've been abused before. In fact, they actively seek out healthy relationships in an effort to avoid further abuse. The problem is that an abused person has a pseudopersonality, which is recognized by psychopaths and narcissists, as I have described above, and abusers then intentionally target the person with a pseudopersonality because they're more vulnerable than others. The predators go after their prey. The abused person doesn't 'attract' abusers. This may appear to be a minor distinction, but it is crucial in terms of recovering from psychological abuse. Of course, the ideal outcome for an abused person is to undo the pseudopersonality and the harm done to them. During this process, they also learn how to identify abusers quickly in order to avoid being caught again.

I see the signs of verbal abuse, what should I do?

When people are in abusive situations and realize that something is wrong, a common reaction is to search the internet for information to help them understand what is going on. They realize they are in an abusive relationship. They begin to investigate that theory and notice signs of verbal abuse. For the reasons stated above, accepting this may take some time. Then it sinks in, and the victim begins to consider what to do about it all. Unfortunately, there are many misleading ideas and suggestions.

'Tell your abuser that what they're doing is upsetting you and that they need to stop. Set boundaries do not let the abuser cross them.'

If you're reading this book, you're probably not in a relationship where your partner said something hurtful, you talked about it with them, they tried to change, and after some trial and error you worked it out between you.

It's much more likely that you've been in an abusive relationship for some time and that you've spent months, if not years, telling your abuser that you don't like what they're doing. But they continue to do it. The abuser has probably broken you down so badly that you realize it's a waste of time to speak up, and speaking back only invites more abuse. You also realize that your abuser is far better at destroying your barriers and pushing you past your limits than you are at establishing them.

Many of these books will also mention the idea that most abusers are psychopaths or narcissists. As a result, negotiating with them is a waste of time. Telling them exactly what irritates you is simply providing them with information that they'll use directly against you at the first opportunity, and the truth is that no matter what you do, they will not change, no matter how much they promise you...

The best thing you can do if you notice signs of verbal abuse in your relationship is to leave. And as quickly as possible.

But, you may be wondering, what if my partner is one of those who has difficulty expressing emotions and may be able to change? Even so, the break will be beneficial. You have the opportunity to settle down, free of abuse, to reflect on your situation, and to decide what to do about it.

While we're on the subject of abusers, it's not necessary to have the abuser diagnosed as a psychopath in order to fully recover. If it looks like a duck, sounds like a duck, and acts like a duck, you don't need to test its DNA in order to treat it as a duck. If the abuser talks like a psychopath, acts like a psychopath, and uses manipulation techniques like a psychopath, you can safely treat him or her as a psychopath. In fact, treating them as a psychopath is the safest thing you can do for yourself!

"But there are children, and I want to stay for their sake," is another frequently cited reason for staying. If one partner in a relationship is abused, especially if the abuser is a psychopath, the children will be abused as well, and the best thing to do is to leave. When the children are with the victim, they will have time away from the abuser. In the best-case scenario, while the adult is recovering from verbal abuse and undoing the pseudopersonality, they can teach the children how to undo their pseudopersonalities as well. As a result, the children are less likely to become easy targets for psychopaths and narcissists later in life.

When you leave the relationship, you are no longer subjected to the manipulator's 24 hour abuse. In many cases, the abuser attempts to maintain control and dominance through email, phone, and social media. However, blocking these routes is much easier than blocking face-to-face conversations. The more contact you have with the abuser, the easier it is for them to reinforce your pseudopersonality. Moving away is usually the best option, though it comes with its own set of complications.

Being away from the manipulator also enables you to rest. It allows you to catch your breath. It allows you to reflect. It allows you to learn because there is so much to learn...

Undoing the Pseudopersonality

Undoing the pseudopersonality and the abuser's damage requires learning about influence, manipulation, narcissists, and psychopaths. It is an educational process in which you learn about the techniques used against you and how these techniques affected your emotions, thinking, decision making, and behaviors. It is critical to be able to recognize mind control techniques in various contexts and recognize them in your own situation.

Many of your beliefs must be unwound and replaced with beliefs that are more beneficial to you. Many of the imposed behavioral patterns must be undone. Many people must relearn that it is okay to make mistakes, how to make their own decisions again, and how to prioritize their own physical and mental well-being.

And as the pseudopersonality fades, the individual's own personality, their own identity, is once again permitted to develop and grow because the individual's development was effectively halted while they were subjected to verbal abuse. This is no small task, and it will take 12 to 18 months to complete under the supervision of a specialist in this field. People who decide to go it alone take much longer, and it is not possible to completely undo a pseudopersonality on their own. Because of the nature of mind control, victims are frequently unable to question the things that they need to question.

It is not always an easy process to go from first noticing signs of verbal abuse to fully recovering. Recognizing how much another person was controlling you is not a pleasant experience, especially if you loved and trusted this person. Getting rid of the pseudopersonality and regaining control of your own life, on the other hand, is always worthwhile. Always.

When going through a recovery, the assistance of an expert is invaluable. It will save you time, energy, money, and heart ache.